IMAGES
of America

BERLIN

IMAGES
of America

BERLIN

Renney E. Morneau
Berlin and Coos County Historical Society

ARCADIA

First printed in 1998.

Published by Arcadia Publishing,
an imprint of Tempus Publishing, Inc.
2 Cumberland Street
Charleston, SC 29401

Printed in Great Britain.

Library of Congress Catalog Card Number: 98-88052

For all general information contact Arcadia Publishing at:
Telephone 843-853-2070
Fax 843-853-0044
E-Mail sales@arcadiapublishing.com

For customer service and orders:
Toll-Free 1-888-313-2665

Visit us on the internet at http://www.arcadiapublishing.com

To Mrs. Mary McKee Moffett and the Late Dr. Irving F. Moffett,
Whose Generosity and Humility Exemplify
the Goodness of the People of Berlin.

CONTENTS

ACKNOWLEDGMENTS

The sources for the images used in this compilation were taken primarily from the Berlin and Coos County Historical Society's vast archives. Various souvenir booklets of Berlin, including *The Business and Industrial Edition* of 1912 and the *Berlin Centennial Book* of 1929, were also utilized. Original Brown Company photographs, many of which graced the publication known as the *Brown Company Bulletin*, also proved to be an invaluable resource. High school yearbooks also helped piece together details of classmates from long ago.

The author/compiler would like to thank the Berlin and Coos County Historical Society for its willingness in approving this endeavor. A special note of gratitude is extended to Mr. and Mrs. Donald Leclerc, without whom none of this would have been possible.

I wish to give special thanks to the following: Mrs. Mary Moffett, Miss Ann R. McKee, Mrs. Louise B. Morneau, Mrs. Doris S. Blanchette, Mr. and Mrs. George L. Ramsey, Ms. Linda Laperle, Androscoggin Valley Hospital, Mrs. Vina Gorham, Mrs. Gorham's Antiques, Mr. Donald Provencher, Miss Dorothy Eichel and Mr. John Davis, the Gorham Historical Society, Mr. and Mrs. Oscar R. Hamlin, Mr. and Mrs. Walter Nadeau, Mr. and Mrs. Bud Leavitt, Mrs. Marion Labnon, Mr. and Mrs. Howard Hawkins, Mrs. Sylvia Evans, Mrs. Josephine Routhier, the late Mr. Roger P. Cooper, Miss Rita Laverdiere, Mr. and Mrs. Joseph Labonte, Mr. and Mrs. James Marquis, Mr. and Mrs. Leon Parent, Mr. and Mrs. Lionel R. Parent, Mr. and Mrs. Harvey Jeffrey, Mr. Otis Bartlett, Mrs. Frederick Prince Sr., Mrs. Beth Isaacson Sanschagrin, Mr. Maurice Lavertue, Mrs. Lois Beaudoin, Mrs. Jean Louis Naud, Mr. Maurice Leclerc, Mr. and Mrs. Lucien Blais, Mr. Richard P. Bosa, Mrs. Judy James, Mr. Maurice Dumais, Mrs. Nancy Lee Brown Snow, Mrs. Clara Oleson, Mr. Sherman Spears, Mrs. Lucille Baillargeon, Fr. Maurice Lacroix, St. Joseph Parish, Sr. Irene Comtois, the Sisters of Presentation of Mary, Mr. and Mrs. Wayne Thompson, Mr. and Mrs. Michael M. Cole, Mr. and Mrs. Ezelbert J. Guay, the Morneau family, Mr. and Mrs. Albert Morneau, Mrs. Reinette Brown Morneau, Mrs. Germaine Saucier, Mrs. Simonne Goudreau, the Kelley family, White Mountain Lumber, Mr. and Mrs. Frank H. Chappell, Mr. Roger Godbout, Smith and Town Printers, Mr. Bertrand E. Bryant and Mr. B. Edward Bryant, Bryant Funeral Homes, Mr. Michael A. and Mr. Raymond N. Patry, Fleury-Patry Funeral Homes, Mr. Paul Charest, Morning Lane Photography, Chief Paul Fortier and Fire Fighter William Maddalena, the Berlin Fire Department, Capt. Walter Nadeau, the Berlin Police Department, Mr. Albin D. Johnson, Berlin Water Works, Mrs. Yvonne Thomas, the Berlin Public Library, Mrs. Barbara Guay, Mr. Richard West, Bob Duncan Photography, Mrs. Arlene Lambert, Mrs. Jane Pulsifer Lambert, Judge and Mrs. Wallace Anctil, Miss Lepha Pickford, Mr. and Mrs. Lionel Fortier, Mr. and Mrs. Leopold Langlois, Mr. Norman Richards, Mount Forist Studio, Mr. and Mrs. George Dumont, and Mrs. and Mrs. Rick McKenzie.

INTRODUCTION

The City that Trees Built, the Paper City, and Hockey Town U.S.A. are all expressions that have been used to describe Berlin, the only city in the largest and most northerly of the New Hampshire's counties, Coos. From its humble beginnings as a chartered township called Maynesboro in 1774, to its incorporation as the City of Berlin in 1897, Berlin's history has been a fascinating and unique journey.

Berlin's fate was sealed in the natural abundance of great forests and unlimited industrial potential presented by such awesome waterpower. The Androscoggin River proved a logical choice for the establishment of mills. Sawed pulp logs could be directed and floated through a network of lakes and rivers, meandering through virgin forests in Maine and New Hampshire while making their long journey to the Berlin mills. Once a quiet hamlet, pastoral in certain respects, fate and location would destine Berlin to take its place among the industrial cities of the Northeast. Fueling the need for progress and productivity, immigrants from every country imaginable would come to toil and persevere in the wood industry. All left their imprints on the community, each with their different talents, techniques, and traditions. Together, whether loggers, farmers, mill workers, or entrepreneurs, their visions all culminated in charting Berlin's future.

Without the Brown Company there is little doubt that Berlin could have been the success that it was. The Brown Company of yesteryear was the livelihood of the community, with a research department that was unparalleled in its brilliance. The Nibroc Paper Towel, brainchild of the late W.E. Corbin, was patented here and is still sold all over the world. Bermico Pipe, constructed of paper and impregnated with tar, was used to protect electrical conduits and was also used as drainage pipe before the advent of PVC pipe. Kodak photographic paper was also made here. Kream of Krisp, the precursor of Crisco lard, was also developed in Berlin.

With time, the Brown Company would pass from ownership of the Brown family to conglomerates such as Gulf and Western, the James River Corporation, and, later, Crown Vantage. Memories of the Brown family would forever remain nostalgic. They are remembered for charitable efforts and their noble gentility. With time, the research department would be no longer. Log drives and the men associated with them would be replaced by wood trucks delivering their precious cargo to the mill. Modern advances, technology, and global competition would gradually place pressures on the paper industry. The demise of the International Paper Company during the Depression and the current downsizing of the Berlin/Gorham Crown Vantage Mill would have an inevitable effect on the community. Through it all, those who provided their raw labor to run the mills, to fell the great trees, and to toil on river drives were also the families who defined Berlin. They were the architects of our community, the inheritors and precursors of continuing ethnic traditions. They were the founders of our churches, schools, banks, businesses, and social organizations.

The elements of paper and lumber production, while providing the primary emphasis for growth and success in earlier years, also helped to spur private business expansion. Entrepreneurs accepted the challenge of the growing bilingual populace, meeting a multitude and variety of consumer demands.

There is a story to be told about Berlin, one of fascination and pride. This is a multifaceted community, its heritage reflected by different languages and cultures, by various occupations and backgrounds culminating in a brilliance unsurpassed in character. The transition from one era to another would not be without its share of challenges. Ultimately, Berlin would always prepare for the unknown by never leaving behind the struggles of the past.

French, Norwegian, Swedish, Russian, Lebanese, Syrian, Irish, Jewish, Finnish, Italian, English, Danish, Polish, and German immigrants would all coalesce to structure a framework of fortitude and pride. Varied as their backgrounds were, Berlin's immigrants all blended to create a brilliant and colorful composite. The cultural flavors, ethnic colors, and work ethic of Berlin's people will always symbolize the mold that we evolved from when our immigrant forefathers came here. The symbol of our community and the interweaving of our cultures is like that of a beautifully detailed Persian rug reflecting the beauty of its colors much like that of our northern hillsides and valleys along the Androscoggin River in autumn.

One

ETCHES OF YESTERYEAR

BERLIN FALLS! Little could one have imagined that this scenic, naturally rugged valley with its awesome waterpower would lead to the development of the wood and paper industries in Berlin, New Hampshire. This scene, taken in 1882, is reminiscent of a simpler time before the onset of industrial development.

A panoramic view of the International Paper Mill Complex, framed by the natural beauty of Mount Washington, by Osgood Studios of Berlin. The Glen Manufacturing Company was organized in 1885, and was purchased by the International Paper Company in 1898.

A river's edge view of the rock cliffs of the Androscoggin River. Note the swift current of the water as it makes its way past the mills, enshrouded by Mount Madison.

Hamming it up for the camera. From left to right, with billboards and the International Paper Co. clock tower in the background, are G. Ross, R. Riva, D. Beaudoin, L. Hodgdon, C. Wilson, F. King, B. Reagan, and P. Beaudoin.

A work crew of the Forest Fibre Company, Berlin, New Hampshire, 1880s. The Forest Fibre Company, owned by H.H. Furbish, started in 1877. It went out of business in the early 1890s.

$500. REWARD.

WHEREAS:---The Selectmen of Berlin, New Hampshire, have offered a reward of $300.00, being the statutory limit, for the apprehension and delivery to the Sheriff of Coos County, the person or persons, who, on the morning of the 17th inst. attempted to destroy the lives of E. J Bonett and his family, and also the property used and occupied by him.

Now, THEREFORE, we the undersigned citizens of said Berlin, hereby agree and promise to pay a further sum of FIVE HUNDRED DOLLARS to any person, or persons who will furnish evidence which shall result in the conviction of the persons who committed the crime above described.

BERLIN, N. H., October 18, 1890.

James W. Parker,	J. M. Lavin,
R. N. Chamberlin,	James Sivret,
Daniel J. Daley,	E. E. Fernald,
S. E. Paine,	John Wilson,
John B. Noyes,	H. J. Brown,
A. M. Stahl,	C. N. Hodgdon,
G. W. Page,	A. H. Gerrish,
J. A. Hodgdon,	L. B. Paine,
C. C. Gerrish & Co.	A. K. Cole.

A REWARD POSTER OF 1890 ASKING FOR EVIDENCE LEADING TO THE APPREHENSION OF WRONGDOERS. Noteworthy of this placard is the fact that Berlin was under the town form of government at this time. Berlin became a city in 1897.

BERLIN SOCIALITES OF THE 1890S. Among those shown here are the Gilberts, the Gerrishs, P. Beaudoin, F. Hodgdon, A.B. Forbush, Dan Daley, J. Letourneau, C. Beattie, A. McNally, B. Bickford, D. Wentworth, and R.N. Chamberlin.

A CHRISTMAS 1895 PORTRAIT. This image shows more of Berlin's leading businessmen. Listed from left to right are E. Abbott, B.B. Bickford, J. Stahl, G.F. Rich, G. Bickford, and J. Balch.

THE BELL BLOCK. This building was located on the corner of Mechanic and Pleasant Streets. The Bell name was associated with livery supplies, livestock, grain, and ice.

A TYPICAL SIGN. A sign like this one was used by customers requesting ice for delivery by the J.F. Bell and Sons Company. The placement of this card in the window informed the deliveryman as to what size ice cake was desired. Prices ranged from 15¢ to 30¢.

A POSTCARD VIEW OF THE **YMCA** BUILDING AND BRIDGE, NEAR COMMUNITY FIELD. The building was erected in 1913. The endeavor was made possible through the efforts of the Berlin Mills Company, the Burgess Company, a bequest by the late W.W. Brown, and the International Paper Company.

A LEGION OF RED CROSS NURSES PARADING ACROSS THE **YMCA** BRIDGE. They were commemorating the end of World War I.

15

SOLDIERS OF WORLD WAR I MARCHING DOWN MAIN STREET, 1919. Doughboys, as they were often referred to at the time, had entered the war effort in 1917.

OLD GLORY. The flag is ceremoniously being carried down Main Street during a victory parade following World War I.

A Knights of Columbus Float. This float was honoring boys returning home. This image was taken near the "narrows," in the vicinity of the future Brown Company Office on Main Street, 1919.

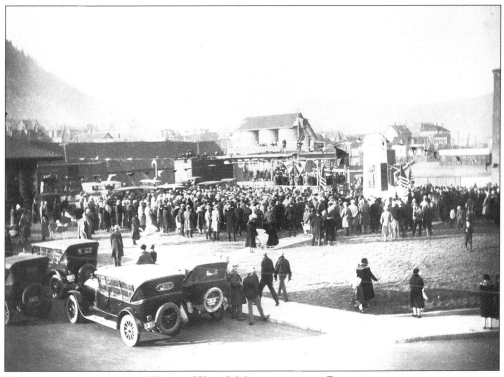

The dedication of the World War I Memorial and Park at the intersection of Pleasant and Mount Forist Streets. The Grand Truck Railroad Station can be seen to the far left, with the Hodgdon Coal silos evident in the center of the picture.

THE POST OFFICE. This stately and architecturally pleasing building was situated at the corner of Main and Mason Streets. Constructed in 1917, its neighbor, Berlin City Hall (constructed in 1913), can be seen to the right.

Main Street, North End, Berlin, N. H.

DAYS OF A BYGONE ERA. This image shows horse and buggy traffic on Main Street near the Gem Theatre.

THE H. WERTHEIM STORE. It was located in the central part of Main Street near the Mason Street intersection, across from Berlin City Hall.

A NOSTALGIC MAIN STREET SCENE. This picture was taken looking south from the Mason Street intersection, before the era of the automobile.

A YESTERYEAR SCENE OF A BUSTLING MAIN STREET WITH HORSE AND BUGGY TRAFFIC NEAR THE GERRISH BLOCK. The Whitcomb Brothers street clock (in the shape of a pocket watch) can be seen outside their establishment.

THE GERRISH BLOCK. This building once housed C.C. Gerrish, E.N. Whitcomb, and G.A. St. Germain D.D.S. It also housed the F.W. Woolworth Company from 1926 to 1994.

THE BERLIN BUSINESS DISTRICT FROM GERRISH BLOCK TO GREEN SQUARE IN 1905. Trolley tracks are evident in this picture. The advent of the automobile was yet to come.

AN 1890S VIEW OF LOWER MAIN STREET LOOKING TOWARD GREEN SQUARE FROM THE F. GLINES BOARDINGHOUSE. This district would change rapidly over the years due to numerous fires and redevelopment.

THE STAFF OF THE STAHL-CLARK STORE. Here they are posing for the shutterbug, near the turn of the century.

THE STOREFRONT OF THE STAHL-CLARK CLOTHING STORE IN 1920. In 1935 the store was purchased by the Labnon family.

A STAHL-CLARK COMPANY PARADE FLOAT CELEBRATING 50 YEARS IN BUSINESS, AROUND 1920.

A 1960 ADVERTISEMENT OF THE LABNON DEPARTMENT STORE. The ad features both the family founders and then-current owners. The Stahl-Clark business was purchased and expanded by the Labnon family. Shown here are Issac, Michael, Ralph (Navy), Morris, Philip, and Emily Labnon. Missing from the advertisement is Daniel Labnon. The Labnon family is legendary for its ownership of the Town and Country Motor Inn in nearby Shelburne, NH.

A VIEW OF POST OFFICE SQUARE WITH A TROLLEY IN SIGHT, BERLIN, NEW HAMPSHIRE, **1916.** Old City National Bank is on left.

A FUTURISTIC SCENE OF BERLIN BY AN IMAGINATIVE ARTIST, 1920S, GREEN SQUARE.

CITY GARAGE COMPANY PERSONNEL POSING WITH NEW BUICK, 1920S. The business was owned by Messrs. Gosselin and Ramsey.

A 1927 FLOOD SCENE OF PLEASANT STREET LOOKING NORTH. Both St. Anne's steeple and the Berlin Fire Department tower can be seen in the distance.

GUAY AND DROUIN'S MEN'S STORE WINDOW WITH A HUNTING THEME, 1940S. The establishment was owned by Mr. Ezelbert Guay and Mr. Albert Drouin. A store noted for its fine quality and service, the proprietors exemplified courtly gentlemen-like manners. The business remained on Berlin's Main Street until 1990, having changed ownership in the late 1970s to Mr. and Mrs. Alfred Arsenault.

A 1950S VIEW OF MAIN STREET NEAR CITY HALL. The image highlights the Dumais Taxi Fleet of vehicles. The business was owned and operated by Mr. and Mrs. Emilien Dumais and their son Maurice. Also in the picture is Jacobs Insurance and Smitty's Smoke Shop.

Two

REMINISCENCES OF THE BROWN COMPANY

A PANORAMIC VIEW OF THE BROWN COMPANY FROM THE EARLY PART OF THE 20TH CENTURY. The image depicts the broad encompassing aspects the mill was known for. Photographed from the northern part of town, every element vital to the mill's existence is here. The Androscoggin River, with its chain of boom piers and boom logs, ensured that the precious cargo of wood would make its way to the multi-faceted operations of the complex. Smoke rising from the stacks demonstrates the viability of the community and its well being.

Mr. W.W. Brown, FOUNDER OF THE BROWN COMPANY. Once known as the Berlin Mills Company, the corporation began in 1852 as the H. Winslow Company. The architect of the Brown Company, Mr. W.W. Brown purchased the controlling interest in the Berlin Mills Company in 1888 and was responsible for building the Burgess Sulphite Mill, the Riverside Paper Mill, the Electro-Chemical plant, and the Cascade Mill.

Mr. O.B. Brown, RESIDENT MANAGER OF MANUFACTURING AND RESEARCH OF THE BROWN COMPANY, 1920S. He was the son of Mr. W.W. Brown.

Mr. W.R. Brown, REVERED MANAGER OF BROWN COMPANY WOODLANDS AND AVID BREEDER OF WORLD-RENOWNED ARABIAN HORSES. He was also a son of Mr. W.W. Brown. Mr. W.R. Brown's research and techniques in both of these beloved areas culminated in his writing extensively on both subjects.

Mr. D.P. Brown. Son of Mr. W.W. Brown, he worked with his brothers, Mr. O.B. Brown and Mr. W.R. Brown. He was responsible for pulp and paper production until 1932.

29

A SOUTHERN NANNY HOLDING GORDON, ONE OF O.B. BROWN'S CHILDREN. Mr. O.B. Brown and his wife, Carline Lewis Gordon Brown, had three children—Gordon, Wentworth, and Caroline Lewis. Mrs. O.B. Brown was a lady of Georgian extraction. Being a lady of southern nobility and affluence, her father, General Gordon, fought for the Confederacy under General Robert E. Lee.

THE RESIDENCE OF O.B. BROWN AND FAMILY ON CHURCH STREET. The Brown name still conjures nostalgic stories of its most respected and benevolent family.

LADIES OF THE CASCADE TOWEL ROOM IN 1922.

GALS FROM THE TOWEL ROOM AT THE CASCADE MILL. They are posing with their Nibroc Towel float in the 1920 parade. Nibroc Towels were named for their developer, Mr. William Corbin.

A VIEW OF A PULP WOODPILE. This was known as the "quarry pile." A conveyer shows the ascent of logs to the top in 1950.

A WELL-DESERVED REST NEAR THE "QUARRY PILE." This moment occurred after these employees had finished the arduous job of shoveling out the conveyer and related area after a fierce February 1958 snowstorm.

A YOUNG LADY POSING ON LOGS NEAR THE CONVEYER TO THE "QUARRY PILE."

KREAM KRISP GIRLS NEAR A LOG CONVEYER, NORTH PULP PILE, 1920. Kream Krisp, forerunner of Crisco cooking lard, was developed by the Brown Company. Kream Krisp was developed when hydrogen gas was brought into contact with peanut oil extractions, hardening it to a lard or butter consistency.

Mr. Roger P. Cooper. This longtime river driver and diver for the Brown Company Power Department prepares for a dive in August of 1957.

The last of a breed! The Brown Company River Crew poses one last time on November 6, 1964. Pictured from left to right are Messrs. Chasse, Daley, Cadorette, Cooper, Johnson, and Bourassa. With pick poles in hand they salute a soon-to-be-bygone era as river drives become history.

THE GROUNDS OF THE OLD BERLIN MILLS SAWMILL COMPLEX IN 1890. Both the Congregational Church of Christ and the Brown Company House can be seen to the right of the photograph.

A BERLIN MILLS RAILWAY LOCOMOTIVE WITH LOADING AND STICKING CAR CONTAINING 39,100 FEET OF LUMBER. This was the largest shipment ever with one car. Delivery was slated for the Brown Company Wharf in Portland, Maine, on April 29, 1925.

A MAINTENANCE CREW OF THE BURGESS SULFITE MILL, WITH SUPERVISORS, C. 1903. The newly constructed Ste. Anne's Catholic Church can be seen towering above the scene.

Berlin, N.H.,
Burgess Sulphite Fibre Co.,-The largest Sulphite Fibre Mill in the World

THE BURGESS SULFITE FIBRE MILL. At that time it was known as the largest of its kind in the world.

A Cascade Mill train crew with Charles Manuel, O. Wheeler, Louis Frechette, and Matthew Gogan.

An old Derby Engine in the lower yard at the Burgess Mill. Pictured from left to right are J. McLellan, Jack Johnson, and John McLellan.

THE BROWN COMPANY HOUSE IN FULL REGALIA FOR THE VISIT OF PRES. DWIGHT D. EISENHOWER IN 1955. Used as a boardinghouse for many years, the building went through the transitions of housing Brown Company guests to housing mill managers in later years. Built in 1853, the residence is now the home of the Northern Forest Heritage Park.

THE HEINE BOILER HOUSE COMPLEX, LOCATED IN THE BURGESS MILL, WITH ITS STAFF IN THE EARLY 1900S.

CASCADE MILLWRIGHTS.
Pictured from left to right are
P. Toppy, A. Sevigny, W.
Desrochers, F. Andrews, and A.
Lessard.

A 1926 PROMOTIONAL PHOTOGRAPH. Employees demonstrate a newly improved electric
power saw.

A panoramic view of crib work construction, taken on September 23, 1920. The

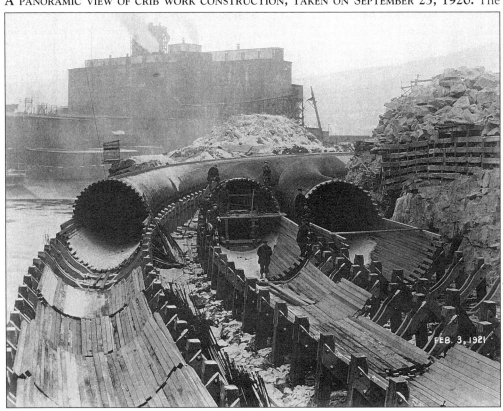

FEB. 3, 1921

The construction of wooden penstock trio with Burgess Sulfite Mill as a backdrop, February 3, 1921.

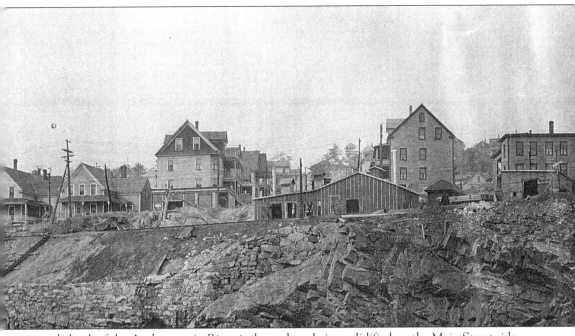

westerly bank of the Androscoggin River is shown here being solidified on the Main Street side.

THE NEW POWER PLANT CONSTRUCTION. This image shows the Coffer Dam with l'Hopital St. Louis and Success Street in the background, July 21, 1920.

BROWN COMPANY CHEMICAL ENGINEER O.R. HAMLIN AT WORK, 1950S.

Left to right, RN's Juliette Lepage, Cecile Parent, Victoria Sullivan, Lydia O'Connell

THANKS GIRLS!

We're proud of our industrial nurses and the part they play in our over-all operations.

By efficiently providing our employees with prompt and courteous attention in matters pertaining to personal health and physical well-being, they are contributing to our company's future success.

When an industrial nurse hands out aspirin to "relieve" a headache, she also goes to work seeking "cure" for that headache. She may find it in a personal condition in the employee's home or in some phase of his working conditions.

Wherever she finds it, so long as she does so and helps to correct the condition, she is making an invaluable contribution to our company's production and the well-being of our employees.

We salute the thousands of nurses working day and night in American industry, ministering to the health and well-being of employees, and very often, curing "headaches" for industry itself.

Berlin, NEW HAMPSHIRE

BROWN COMPANY INDUSTRIAL NURSES IN A 1950S PRESS RELEASE. Pictured from left to right are Juliette Lepage, Cecile Parent, Victoria Sullivan, and Lydia O'Connell.

Three
A Cultural Legacy

THE OLESON CITY BAND. The band, comprised primarily of Scandinavian Brown Company employees, poses in Cascade Park on Labor Day in 1903. Culturally, Berlin was representative of much of the country, which became enthralled with bandstand concerts and the sheer enjoyment of pursuing such leisure activities. Other bands and symphonic groups entertained friends and family alike in places such as the Clement Opera House and the subsequent Albert Theatre.

A Junior Nansen Ski Club competitor. A determined expression envelops this young man as he readies himself for competition.

Spectators lining upper Main Street. These people are making their way to the Winter Carnival and ski-jumping festivities.

A BIRD'S-EYE VIEW. This image captured two ski jumpers launching from the old jump overlooking Paine's Pasture in the early 1920s.

A FRONTAL VIEW OF THE OLD SMALLER JUMP NEAR THE TOP OF TWELFTH STREET. The spectators anxiously anticipate the next jumper.

THE NEW NANSEN SKI JUMP. Situated on the Berlin/Milan line, it was constructed in 1936. Hosting some of the finest ski jumpers in the world, much of the organization and planning behind the events would not have been possible without the diligent efforts of the late Alf Halvorson.

A PROMOTIONAL PHOTOGRAPH OF THE OLESONS AT BOSTON GARDEN IN 1940. Pictured from left to right are Spike, Pearl, and Alton Oleson.

FLYING SOLO, NORDIC STYLE. This silhouette captured Sherman Spears, a notable and distinguished ski jumper, in his first jump off the new Nansen Ski Jump in 1937. Unparalleled in bravery, jumpers of his caliber battled elements ranging from harsh wind currents to subzero temperatures. Kenneth Fysh and Leon Costello were also notable in this event, among many others.

A PARADE SCENE OF A TIN LIZZIE AND FIRE TRUCK NEAR THE YMCA BRIDGE. The domed public library can be seen on the far right. This scene is reminiscent of the strong patriotic sentiment of the day.

A FRONTAL VIEW OF THE BERLIN PUBLIC LIBRARY AFTER ITS COMPLETION IN 1904.

LIBRARIANS GERMAINE LEBLANC THOMPSON, LOTTIE SHERIDAN, AND FERNANDE BLAIS. They are posing at the return desk of the Berlin Public Library.

LIBRARIANS GLADYS FARRINGTON, YVONNE THOMAS, SHERRY MORIN, LOUISE BIRT, AND INEZ HAMLIN IN A MORE CONTEMPORARY POSE.

The Albert Theatre, Berlin, N. H.

A FRONTAL VIEW OF THE ALBERT THEATRE IN 1911. Situated on a portion of the site occupied by the former Clement Opera House, it was owned and operated by Albert Croteau. Many still remember the playing of the Wurlitzer Theatre Organ for the many silent films and orchestral productions by Ward Steady.

THE BERLIN SYMPHONY ORCHESTRA WITH PERFORMERS IN BACKDROP AT THE ALBERT THEATRE IN 1927. The conductor was Dr. E.R.B. McGee, a mayor of Berlin.

THE BURGESS MINSTRELS, A RELIEF ASSOCIATION OF THE BROWN COMPANY COMPRISED OF EMPLOYEES. 1917. The productions would be performed every year to raise money for injured fellow coworkers. Pictured from left to right in parade attire on Emery Street from High Street are H.T. Raeburn, F.W. Rahmanop, J.P. Fagin, and J. McKinnon. The Moffett House, once known as the residence for managers of the International Paper Company, can be seen to the left.

THE BURGESS MINSTRELS. Here they are marching down Main Street near the corner of Main and Mason Streets in 1914.

TOUS LES CITOYENS DE LANGUE FRA

zo N. Labonté
SHERIF
du comté
COOS

Eli J. King
Maître de
Poste

G. A. Cournoyer
Greffier
de la
ville

Roland J. Brideau
Commissaire des
travaux publics
de la ville

René Gagnon
Conseiller
Quartier
1

Alfred J. Gauvin
Conseiller
Quartier
4

Roméo Désilets
Conseiller
Quartier
2

Alb. A. Des
Conseille
Quartie
4

D'OFFRIR NOS MEILLEURS

RO-JOY

Sealtest
ICE CREAM

A. Gosselin
Gérant
Berlin, N. H.

MEILLEURS

VOEUX

À NOS

COMPATRIOTES

Joseph Dumont
Propriétaire
Berlin Second
Hand Store
133, rue Cole — Tél. 832

Amédée Routhier
Propriétaire
East Side Drug
Rue Mason

BEAULAC'S

IDEAL

DAIRY

R. J. Boulanger
propriétaire
Tél. 280
109, rue State

Léon O. Trottier
Propriétaire et gérant
Pharmacie "Rexal"
Wilson
23, rue Main — Tél. 273

**HOM
A
ANC**

OTRE FÊTE PATRONALE

e Ern. Dubois
Propriétaire
s Remnant Shop
e Main — Tél. 1545

J. A. Vaillancourt
Lt. Comm.

Maurice L. Vaillancourt
U. S. N. R.

J. A. Vaillancourt Insurance Agency
60ième anniversaire
157, rue Main   Téléphone 124

Pfc. Elzebert F. Guay   **S. 1/c Albert E. Drouin**
Propriétaires
Guay & Drouin's Men's Shop
73-75, rue Main   Téléphone 780

FRANCO-AMÉRICAINS DE LA NOUVE

**THE
OTOR**

BLAIS & AUBIN
WHOLESALE

**SOUHAITS
SINCÈRES
À**

**CITY
DISTRIBUTING
CO.**
Distributeurs
des produits

**Toussai
Bakin**

A CENTERFOLD FROM A NEWSPAPER CALLED LE JOURNAL. This Franco-American newspaper published in Berlin, New Hampshire, provided a wonderfully fitting tribute to the Franco-

AISE À BERLIN, NOUS SOMMES DÉSIREU

Sinai J. Demers

SOUHAITS SINCÈRES À TOUS

MEILLEURS VOEUX À NOS COMPATRIOTES

E. Morin
MAIRE DE LA VILLE

R. J. Morneau
Conseiller Quartier 1

Léo R. Leblanc
Conseiller Quartier 4

Sinaï J. Demers
Conseiller Quartier 1

Edmond Chaloux
Conseiller Quartier 2

Paul F. Jeannotte
Percepteur du Revenu de l'Intérieur fédéral

Arthur Boulanger
Agent fiscal du comté COOS

Art. J. Berg
Procureur du comté COOS

SOUHAITS EN CE JOUR DI

MEILLEURS VOEUX À NOS COMPATRIOTES

Nos souha sincères

Emma

Restaura and CANDY SHOPPE

Herman E. Miles
Président

Joseph Morris
Trésorier

Compliments de

Georges J. Daigle
Propriétaire
Daigle Motors Inc.
Rue Pleasant — Tél. 1550

Emma Beau

Propriétaire
249, rue Main—Tél

C. N. HODGDON CO.
Marchands de chauffage depuis 1885.

Gédéon J. Croteau

LA SAINT-JEAN-BAPTIST

Roméo Morin

Joseph Morin
Fondateur

Roland Morin

Arthur Massey

Florence Mas

MORIN SHOE STORE
301, rue MAIN

Propriétaires
FLORENCE'S BEAUTY SHO
Téléphone 887-W 53, rue Church

LETERRE, RALLIONS-NOUS...

SON'S RAGE

PARENT & CHAGNON

BELL Hardware

Salon Funéraire

City Wholesale

Gossel

American citizens of Berlin. Noted businessmen and city officials of Francophone heritage saluted the celebration of the feast known as Saint-Jean Baptiste. This was published in 1945.

MORE BURGESS MINSTRELS. These ladies in a classic 1911 pose did their part to raise money for the Relief Association in their affiliation to the Burgess Minstrels.

A KIWANIS CLUB CHARTERING BANQUET. This group photograph was taken at the YMCA Building on February 8, 1927.

Msgr. Patrick E. Walsh, assembly of the Fourth Degree Knights of Columbus, October 23, 1955.

A group photograph of the 34th annual Elks Club convention. The club was a respected social organization in Berlin for many years.

LE ROI DES MONTAGNES, WITH BLACK AND WHITE UNIFORMS, NEAR CEDAR POND ON A WINTER OUTING IN 1937. The Snowshoe Club was well noted for its French-Canadian origin and orchestral talents.

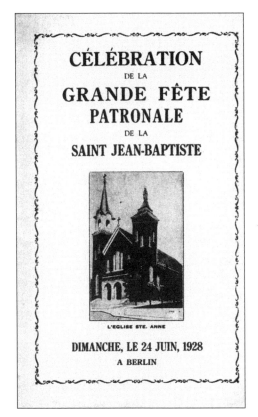

THE FRONT BOOKLET COVER OF THE FRANCO-AMERICAN CATHOLIC CELEBRATION. This celebration was known as La Saint Jean Baptiste. The feast day, a holiday of French-Canadian importance, was celebrated by Franco-American Catholics annually.

Four

PILLARS OF FAITH

HOUSES OF WORSHIP. The Berlin community has always been faithful and devout in its beliefs. The many nationalities and religions were all responsible for paying testament and homage to the Almighty. Different sectors of the city soon boasted beautiful places of worship. The above scene in particular is representative of the Franco-Americans, who through their perseverance and dedication were responsible for the erection of l'Eglise Ste. Anne in 1900, l'Academie St. Regis in 1911, and the establishment of l'Hopital St. Louis in 1905.

REV. NARCISSE COURNOYER, ONE OF THE EARLY PASTORS OF LA PAROISSE STE. ANNE. His dedication and commitment led to the construction of the first l'Eglise Ste. Anne in 1884. He passed away in 1899.

AN ANTIQUE POSTCARD OF THE NEWLY CONSTRUCTED EDIFICE OF L'EGLISE STE. ANNE AND RECTORY WITH CAMEO PORTRAITS OF REVERENDS LOUIS LAPLANTE AND HENRI BRODEUR AROUND 1905. Reverend LaPlante was responsible for the building of the new Ste. Anne in 1900 and was the major catalyst for the establishment of l'Hopital St. Louis.

MSGR. PATRICK E. WALSH, PASTOR OF ST. KIERAN'S CHURCH FROM 1934 TO 1957. Msgr. Walsh was responsible for many things, among them the new construction of the St. Patrick Elementary School in 1948.

AN ANTIQUE VIEW OF ST. KIERAN'S AT THE TURN OF THE CENTURY WITH CAMEOS OF REVERENDS MACKEY AND HACKETT. The pastor and founder of St. Kieran's Church, Fr. Edward Mackey oversaw and initiated construction of St. Kieran's in 1894 and St. Patrick's School in 1902.

MSGR. ALPHERI LAUZIERE, PASTOR OF LA PAROISSE ST. JOSEPH. A very powerful, capable, and saintly man, he was the first pastor of the newly founded parish in 1941. L'Eglise St. Joseph was built under his direction beginning in 1957. He was instrumental in the construction of St. Joseph School in 1929, the Berlin Catholic Boxing Club, and the establishment of the Notre Dame Arena in 1948.

A VIEW OF ST. JOSEPH CHURCH AND RECTORY AS IT STILL APPEARS TODAY.

MSGR. OMER F. BOUSQUET, PASTOR OF LA PAROISSE L'ANGE GARDIEN LOCATED ON BERLIN'S EAST SIDE. An individual who cared deeply for his community and its people, he was one of the driving forces behind the establishment of the l'Ecole Secondaire Notre Dame, known as Notre Dame High School, as well as the establishment of the Caisse Populaire l'Ange Gardien, known as Guardian Angel Credit Union, with Mr. Joseph Dumont in 1929.

L'EGLISE L'ANGE GARDIEN SITUATED ON SULLIVAN STREET IN THE LATE 1930S. This image was taken at the end of Sunday Mass. It was, and still is, the only Catholic church on the east side of the city.

61

A GROUP OF RIVER DRIVERS SORTING LOGS. St. Paul Lutheran Church and the Norwegian Village are in the background. The church was founded in 1887.

AN 1891 VIEW OF THE NEWLY CONSTRUCTED ST. PAUL LUTHERAN CHURCH. The Scandinavians in this picture were members of Berlin's first Temperance Society.

A WEDDING DAY PHOTOGRAPH OF GARDA (DINASS) HANSEN AT THE ST. PAUL LUTHERAN CHURCH IN 1928. Pictured from left to right are Frida (Dinass) Johnson, Garda (Dinass) Hansen, and Hilma (Dinass) Hansen.

MR. AND MRS. MARTIN HANSEN. They are posing for a family picture with their new automobile at a St. Paul Lutheran family picnic.

THE BETH ISRAEL SYNAGOGUE ON UNITY STREET. Originally a Unitarian church, it served the Jewish community for many years. Members of the flourishing Jewish community in Berlin included the Evans, Isaacson, Stahl, Brown, Segal, Rosenberg, Morrison, Nusman, Wertheim, Davis, Abramson, Israel, Brody, Winer, Jacobs, Reisner, and Danneman families.

THE BAR MITZVAH OF ELI ISAACSON. It was held in the downstairs of the synagogue in 1953. Pictured from left to right are the following: (front row) Jeannie Zeltzer and Eli and Mizzie Isaacson; (back row) Sadie, Frederick, Charles, and Sophie Isaacson, and Hyman Zeltzer.

THE ORIGINAL ST. BARNABAS EPISCOPAL CHURCH. The church was constructed in 1889. It burned in 1929, but was replaced by a new stone church.

A VIEW OF THE STONE ST. BARNABAS CHURCH. This was constructed after the 1929 fire. Ste. Anne's Church is in background.

THE CONGREGATIONAL CHURCH OF CHRIST. It is situated near the Brown Company House, and was endowed by the Brown family in its early days. It was founded in 1881.

THE FIRST BAPTIST CHURCH, LOCATED AT THE CORNER OF HIGH AND SCHOOL STREETS.

A VIEW OF THE HOLY RESURRECTION RUSSIAN ORTHODOX CHURCH, LOCATED ON THE CORNER OF PETROGRAD AND RUSSIAN STREETS. It was built in 1915 by the ardent Russian families who came to Berlin in search of a better life. The names of the Tupick, Lavernoich, Snigger, Snitko, Radsky, Buckovitch, Darchick, Kovalik, and Kluchnick families are firmly rooted in Berlin history, as are many others of Russian extraction.

V. Rev. John Kozitsky
Dean

V. Rev. Arcady Piotrowsky
The First Rector and builder of Holy Ressurection Russian Orthodox Church.

The Rev. John Morozoff
Rector

A COLLAGE OF THE PRIESTS OF THE HOLY RESURRECTION ORTHODOX CHURCH.

SKI MASS, AT ST. KIERAN'S CHURCH IN 1937. This concept was the first of its kind in the country and was first held in 1936.

A NOSTALGIC VIEW OF L'ACADEMIE ST. REGIS. It is adorned with red, white, and blue bunting and had a ceremonial arch at entrance reading "Religion and Country" in French.

Five

SHADES OF NOSTALGIA

POISED HIGH ABOVE THE SKYLINE OF BERLIN. As these two young lads can attest, Berlin, this burgeoning hamlet of a paper city, was destined to make its mark. Paper, Berlin's speeding-locomotive industry, was well established by the time this photograph was taken in 1915. Among the timbers of the valley could be found a microcosm virtually unparalleled in ethnic mixture and strong work ethics, second to none in natural resources and human spirit. Both paper mills of the day, the Brown Company and the International Paper Company, can be seen flanking the Androscoggin River drawing their lifeline from the endless toil of felling trees and making paper.

THE GRAND TRUNK RAILROAD STATION AS IT APPEARED IN 1907. This was the third railroad station to be built in this location, the others having succumbed to fire. A fourth stone station would be built here in 1917.

THE EAST SIDE TRAIN STATION ON UNITY STREET IN 1912. Mr. Duval is in his automobile awaiting debarking passengers.

AN OLD DEPICTION OF THE R.A. BROWN TOBACCO AND CONFECTIONERY STORE, WITH A.B. FORBUSH AND SHERIFF BROWN STANDING IN THE ENTRANCE. The A.B. Forbush Jeweler sign is prominently displayed in the left window.

A NOSTALGIC PHOTOGRAPH OF THE A.B. FORBUSH JEWELRY AND WATCH STORE. The personnel stand proudly amongst the varied pocket watches in their window display.

An exquisite interior view of the Wilson Pharmacy. The pharmacy was located at the corner of Main and Mechanic Streets. The business later became the Rexall Pharmacy, and in recent years has been the location of Office Products of Berlin.

The exterior of the drugstore of Norman LaRochelle, LaRochelle's Pharmacy, in 1937. The pharmacy was located on Main Street.

MR. NORMAN LaROCHELLE, PHARMACIST AND PROPRIETOR OF LaROCHELLE'S PHARMACY. Pharmacies were quite numerous during these times. Among them were the East Side Drug Company, Plunkett's Pharmacy, Morneault's Drug Store, Wilson's Pharmacy, M.J. Mullen, and Moffett's Pharmacy.

LaROCHELLE'S PHARMACY SODA FOUNTAIN AND PERSONNEL. Pictured from left to right are Yvette Fauteux, Louis Micucci, Kittie Calais, Sally O'Neill Donnelly, Pearl Dahlson, Audrey Sullivan, and Ethel Gallant Vaillancourt.

MR. GEORGE RAMSEY AND THE ROBICHAUD BOYS. While taking a break from haying on Cates Hill they posed with this farm tedder machine and "Nora," 1940.

CHILDREN POSING FOR THE CAMERA ON CATES HILL, 1925. Pictured from left to right are Jeannette Bisson, Olive Bisson, Alice Bisson, Germaine Bisson, Adeline Bisson, Charlotte Bisson, Helen Bisson, and Irene Bisson.

MOUNTAIN VIEW FARM, CATES HILL. Long known as the Bisson Farm, it was photographed here on Christmas Day in 1925.

MR. PAUL BISSON, PROPRIETOR OF BISSON'S DAIRY. Along with his wife, Yolande, their family, and the George Ramsey family, the farm was the last to operate within the Berlin city limits, closing in 1988.

"**Big Bess.**" This Berlin Public Works snowplow was photographed as it cleared snow from the latest storm in 1936. Manning the truck are Ernest Patrick and Avila Comtois.

A Berlin Public Works crew shoveling Cates Hill Road, 1920s.

THE FIRST BISSON SUGARHOUSE, CATES HILL, IN 1921. The sugarhouse was begun by Lazarre Bisson, changing in ownership through the years to Armand and Juliette Bisson. It is currently operated by Lucien Blais and his family. In 1953 the building shown here was replaced by a more modern sugarhouse.

PAINE'S BRIDGE. This covered bridge was constructed by Daniel Davis in 1857. It spanned the Androscoggin River just north of the present Twelfth Street Bridge.

WATER TRANSMISSION LINE PIPING. It is being loaded onto a horse-drawn sleigh for delivery to the future Kilkenny Godfrey Dam Reservoir, 1920.

WORKERS POSING WITH THE WATER TRANSMISSION LINE. This image was taken during construction of the Godfrey Dam Pipeline, 1920s.

BERLIN PUBLIC WORKS' HORSE-DRAWN WAGON NO. 104. It was being driven by Mr. Wilfrid Lalande in this 1930s image. Mr. Lalande aided in the pipeline project.

THE COMPLETED 5.5-MILE WATER TRANSMISSION MAIN FROM GODFREY DAM TO THE CITY OF BERLIN. Installation was done by men and horses without any heavy equipment.

THE J.P. CHOUINARD ELECTRIC SHOP WITH FAMILY POSING FOR A 1929 BERLIN CENTENNIAL PICTURE.

THE HALLE AND SONS MEAT MARKET, CORNER OF PLEASANT AND MAIN STREETS, C. 1910. The Halles were responsible for developing what is commonly known today as Blanchette's sausage, a special sausage recipe that continues to be enjoyed by many Franco-American families.

THE MAINGUY BROTHERS IN A WORLD WAR II ADVERTISEMENT. Andre J. Mainguy's Meat Market, at 681 First Avenue, later moved to 695 Main Street, where it remained into the 1980s. Mr. Mainguy retired in 1975 and was instrumental in chartering the Berlin Lion's Club. Pictured here are Andre, Leo, Roland, Peter, and Rene Mainguy.

MR. FREDERICK A. PRINCE, PROPRIETOR OF PRINCE'S CORNER MARKET AND IGA FOODLINER. Prince was a respected businessman and community leader and became well known for his humanitarian efforts in aiding the Salvation Army, the Red Cross, and for his benevolence toward his community.

THE MORNEAU SONS. Shown here are Edgar, Rene, Philip, Armand, Albert, Robert, and Roland, in a photograph taken during World War II.

MORNEAU AND SONS MOVERS WITH A TRACTOR-TRAILER AT THE BASE OF MOUNT WASHINGTON. The company was started in 1910 by Joseph and Dorilda Morneau. In addition to their seven sons, the Morneau family also included five daughters—Therese, Cecile, Jeannette, Pauline, and Lucille.

MR. ALBERT J. SAUCIER, PROMINENT INDEPENDENT INSURANCE AGENT AND DISTRIBUTOR OF *LA PRESSE*, A FRENCH NEWSPAPER FROM CANADA. A gentleman of distinguished character and integrity, he was married to the former Marie Louise Blain. They had five children—Paul, Gaston, Rene, Jacqueline, and Colette.

Albert J. Saucier

ASSURANCES GÉNÉRALES

Agent de "LA PRESSE"

283, rue High   Tel. 37   Berlin, N. H.

MR. SAUCIER'S BUSINESS CARD. The card reflects the strong Franco-American culture of the 1920s and 1930s. His office and residence were located at 283–285 High Street. Besides his independent insurance agency affiliations, he sought to promote the fraternal pride of l'Association Canado Americaine and Francophone culture through making the Saint Jean Baptiste Life Insurance policies obtainable to many families that might otherwise not have had the means to purchase insurance. The Saucier Insurance Agency was sold to the Jacobs Insurance Agency after Mr. Saucier passed away in 1956, ending over 50 years in the profession.

THE BARBERSHOP OF GEORGE BOIRE. Mr. Boire is pictured above with Alva Boire and Mr. Denary Halle, the customer seated in chair, on Main Street in 1915.

MR. LAURIER BISSON OF LARRY'S BARBERSHOP, NEAR THE PRINCESS THEATRE ON GREEN SQUARE OPPOSITE THE BERLIN CITY BANK. Mr. Bisson holds the distinction of being the first U.S. Army photographer to develop the pictures of the nuclear attacks on Japan in 1945.

MESSRS. WILFRED COUTURE AND AIME TONDREAU. Tondreau was the mayor of Berlin and proprietor of Tondreau's Barbershop located on East Mason Street. During his tenure as mayor, his establishment became known as "City Hall" to many.

MR. ANTONIO BIRON POSING IN FRONT OF HIS SHOP ON MAIN STREET ACROSS FROM THE LABNON'S DEPARTMENT STORE. Mr. Biron was in business until the late 1980s.

MR. LAURIER "BEE" ROUSSEAU, BERLIN CITY TAX COLLECTOR AND LONGTIME FRENCH ANNOUNCER ON WMOU. He was known for his famous line "Au micro Bee Rousseau."

WMOU RADIO. This station has been the radio voice of the White Mountains since 1945. Radio personalities Bob Barbin, Bob Powell, and Rod Ross are voices well known to Berlin listeners on both sister stations WMOU AM and WXLQ FM. One other radio station also existed in Berlin. WBRL, whose call letters stood for Berlin, signed off in the late 1980s.

In the Mountain Region analytical advertisers use the facilities of

W M O U

**THE RADIO VOICE
OF THE WHITE MOUNTAINS
BERLIN, N. H.**

MR. EMMET J. KELLEY, LONGTIME
INFLUENTIAL DEMOCRATIC PARTY
SUPPORTER AND LOCAL
BUSINESSMAN. He was a national
horseracing commissioner and water
commissioner for the Berlin Water
Works as well as a joint partner with
Emile Napert of the current White
Mountain Lumber Company.

MR. RICHARD GUNN, OWNER AND
GENERAL MANAGER OF THE FORD
AUTO MART LOCATED ON UPPER
MAIN STREET IN BERLIN.
Mr. Gunn was an ardent Republican,
successful businessman, Kiwanian,
Elk's Member, and Berlin Water
Works Commissioner.

THE COOS COUNTY COURTHOUSE AS DECORATED FOR CHRISTMAS IN THE 1930s. It was constructed in 1904, and is located on the westerly side of the Androscoggin River, Main Street.

ATTORNEY ARTHUR O. DUPONT. This practicing attorney for nearly 60 years was the founder of the Dupont and Anctil Law Firm.

ATTORNEY ARTHUR BERGERON SR. OF BERGERON AND HANSON, ATTORNEYS AT LAW. Attorney Bergeron once served as legal counsel for the Brown Company. He served for a time as mayor of Berlin and was a proponent of the Farmer Labor Party.

ATTORNEY ARNOLD HANSON. He is well known for having served with distinction as chairman of the Berlin City Bank Board of Directors.

Mr. and Mrs. George Baillargeon, proprietors of George's Candy Shop. The establishment operated across from the Coos County Courthouse from 1938 until the late 1970s. The large mural which graced the rear wall of their store was painted by local artist and painting contractor Mr. Honore Bergeron.

Mr. Baillargeon decorating chocolate Easter eggs in the 1950s.

EMMA'S CANDY SHOP AND RESTAURANT NEAR THE BERLIN FIRE STATION. The shop was a well-known rendezvous for many after spending an evening at the movies.

THE HILLSIDE MARKET. Known for many years as Major's Store, it was later owned by the Blanchette family. Pictured are Doris, Leo, and Louise Blanchette.

CHANNING AND SYLVIA EVANS, PROPRIETORS OF EVAN'S DEPARTMENT STORE. They were both respected and revered citizens of Berlin. Their contributions to the community spanned the spectrum of religious, fraternal, charitable, and humanitarian sectors.

MR. ELI ISAACSON, PRESIDENT OF ISAACSON STRUCTURAL STEEL INC. He was committed to the betterment of his community and its citizens. His involvement in community affairs is legendary and his dedication to the Republican Party tireless.

92

MR. JOSEPH G. BLAIS, A PROMINENT BERLIN FRANCO-AMERICAN BUSINESSMAN. Blais was involved in the wholesale and merchandising business known by many as the Blais and Aubin Wholesale Company, located at 16 Mechanic Street.

TOUSSAINT BAKERY IN ITS HEYDAY. These makers of Butter Crust Bread were located on the corner of School and Willard Streets. Many still reminisce about the wonderful aromas of their bread and pastries.

THE CONVERSE RUBBER COMPANY AS IT APPEARED IN THE MID-1950S. Located on Jericho Road, the shoe factory employed 950 people in its heyday. Converse closed in 1979.

A TROLLEY CAR BY CITY HALL, MAIN STREET, BERLIN. This car, known as No. 6, is destined for the town of Gorham. Streetcars were replaced by buses in December 1938.

A Berlin Street Railway motor bus. These buses went into service in December of 1938, replacing streetcars.

First Sgt. Frank H. Chappell. He was one of several U.S. Army guards stationed at Camp Stark, a World War II POW camp detaining German soldiers in 1944. Many of the POWs were engaged in woods operations, with much of their labor assisting the paper production in the Berlin/Gorham Mills.

MR. AND MRS. JACK BROWN, PROPRIETORS OF THE BERLIN FLOWER SHOP, LATER KNOWN AS BROWN THE FLORIST, 1922–59. With greenhouses in Gorham, the flower shop was located across from Ste. Anne's Church and then on lower Main Street.

AN EARLY
ADVERTISEMENT OF
BROWN THE FLORIST.

GILL'S FLOWER SHOP, FORMERLY KNOWN AS SMITH GREEN HOUSES. This establishment continues to provide floral tributes to the area's residents in its 98th consecutive year or business. The tradition, passed on from Thomas Gill to his son, is now owned and operated by his granddaughter Barbara.

JOSEPH AND ROSA BOSA OTTOLINI. Mr. Ottolini was responsible for signing the patent of the Farrand Rule in the 1920s. The Ottolini and Bosa families exemplified the strong work ethic of the Italian immigrant families of Berlin's East Side and of the Cascade Hill and Cascade Flats neighborhoods. The Alonzo, Addario, Memolo, Sinibaldi, Costello, Baldassare, Ferrante, Prince, Femia, Catello, Nicoletti, Mosca, Cellupica, Cavagnaro, Dalphonse, Bartoli, and Pisani families are among those with deep roots in Berlin's history.

A FARRAND RULE ADVERTISEMENT. This was the forerunner of the modern tape measure.

RALPH PELOQUIN, HARVEY JEFFREY, AND AL SINIBALDI, CHAMPIONS OF THE BERLIN CATHOLIC BOYS BOXING CLUB. The club was envisioned and guided by Msgr. Alpheri O. Lauziere.

A NORTHERN OIL BASKETBALL TEAM IN THE 1920S. Among the players pictured are Gus Rooney, Maxie Agrodnia, and Forrist Steady.

THE "KING OF THE ANDROSCOGGIN." Off. Fred Landry was photographed here log rolling with a pick pole in hand before spectators in the 1930s.

A KIDDIE DAY PARADE WITH A LION'S CLUB FLOAT MAKING ITS WAY UP MAIN STREET IN 1952. The Dumais Taxi Stand, a pastry shop, and Brown the Florist are all visible in this photograph.

Six

HELPING HANDS

AN EARLY SIDE VIEW OF THE "L'HOPITAL SAINT LOUIS" OR SAINT LOUIS HOSPITAL IN 1905. Pictured with the hospital backdrop is a horse-drawn ambulance owned by Mr. Henry A. St. Laurent, who was also a local funeral director at the time. Pictured behind the ambulance are Mr. St. Laurent and Dr. McGee.

SOEURS DE CHARITE OR SOEURS GRISES, KNOWN AS THE GRAY NUNS OF THE SISTERS OF CHARITY. This order of sisters from St. Hyancithe, P.Q. Canada, administered hospital policies and operations. The above photograph was taken in 1955.

A TYPICAL MAIN STREET HOSPITAL ROOM IN 1920.

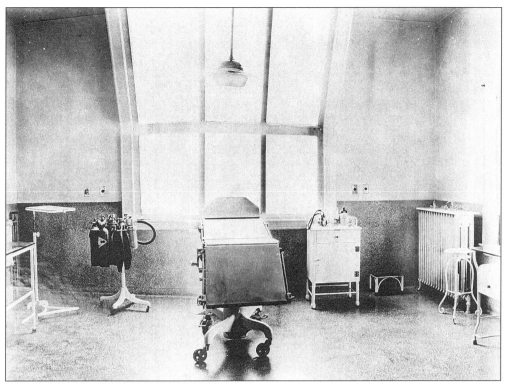

AN OPERATING ROOM OF THE SAINT LOUIS HOSPITAL IN 1923.

NURSING STUDENTS ENJOYING AN EVENING OF LEISURE WHILE STUDYING AT THE ST. LOUIS SCHOOL OF NURSING IN 1942. It operated until 1972.

DR. T.C. PULSIFER. He was a well-known family practitioner in Berlin for many years. He was liked and respected by his colleagues and was very involved in athletic circles.

DRS. JULIUS ISRAEL (BELOW LEFT) AND H.E. WILKINSON (BELOW RIGHT). Doctor Israel immigrated to the United States from Russia after the First World War. Doctor Wilkinson was a noted family physician and practiced at 72 High Street.

Dr. J.E. LaRochelle. This Franco-American physician and surgeon was noted for sporting a fresh boutonniere in his lapel each day. His respected practice lasted until the 1960s.

Dr.s E.J. Thibodeau (below left) and P.A. Dumontier (below right). These Franco-American physicians were quite well known for serving the large French population in Berlin. Dr. Thibodeau practiced into the late 1940s and Dr. Dumontier until the 1980s.

DR. IRVING F. MOFFETT,
OSTEOPATHIC SURGEON AND WELL-
KNOWN PERSONALITY, POSING WITH
HIS BUICK ROADMASTER. His practice
was located at 119 High Street from
1949 to 1993, and in the downtown for
many years previous.

DR. AND MRS. IRVING F. MOFFETT.
Mrs. Moffett's legendary kindness and
generosity led to her donation of her
home to the Berlin and Coos County
Historical Society in 1996 for the
establishment of a museum on local
history.

THE RESIDENCE OF DR. AND MRS. IRVING F. MOFFETT. This house was once the corporate residence of the International Paper Company and home of Mrs. Anna Gross, owner of the Berlin Street Railway. It is now the home of the Berlin and Coos County Historical Society.

Dr. I. F. Moffett
OSTEOPATHIC PHYSICIAN AND SURGEON
BY APPOINTMENT ONLY
Hours: 9 a. m. to 12 noon, 2 p. m. to 5 p. m.

Osteopathy, Obstetrics, Skin Diseases, Rectal and Pelvic Diseases, Epilepsy, Infantile Paralysis, Varicose Veins, the Non-Operative Treatment of Hernia, Ear, Eye, Nose and Throat, Glasses Fitted, Removal of Tonsils and Adenoids without Ether, Pain or Hemmorrhage, Finger Surgery in Catarrhal Deafness. Treatment of Corns, Callouses, Ingrown Nails, Athletic Feet, Arch Troubles and all Foot Ailments.

AN ADVERTISING PLACARD OF DR. I.F. MOFFETT, LISTING HIS SPECIALTIES.

Dr. Ira Allen Tucker

DR. IRA TUCKER. Tucker was a homeopathic physician from Milan, NH, who cared for indigent patients in the city of Berlin during Berlin's early years.

THE SAINT LOUIS HOSPITAL IN 1938. The expansion of 1938 was the second in its 33-year existence.

DR. R.H. McVETTY, A LONGTIME BERLIN PHYSICIAN WHO PRACTICED OUT OF HIS OFFICE AT 147 HIGH STREET. He was revered and liked by many and was the public school athletic physician for some time.

DR. E.M. DANAIS. Originally of Manchester, NH, he served Berlin residents for many years. Arriving in the 1940s, this Franco-American doctor became well known for taking care of his East Side clientele.

THE BERLIN FIRE DEPARTMENT'S 1905 HORSE-DRAWN AMOSKEAG STEAM FIRE PUMPER.

THE ICE-LADEN REMAINS OF BERLIN'S NATIONAL BANK, GREEN SQUARE. The blaze that destroyed the bank happened in the early 1900s. When this photograph was taken, the temperature was 30 degrees below zero.

A GROUP PORTRAIT OF BERLIN FIRE DEPARTMENT PERSONNEL IN THE EARLY 1900S.

A HORSE-DRAWN BERLIN FIRE DEPARTMENT LADDER TRUCK FROM YESTERYEAR.

LADDER #1 WITH PERSONNEL AND MOUNT FORIST IN BACKGROUND, 1940, NEAR THE BERLIN FIRE STATION. The Strand Theater is to the right of this photograph.

BERLIN FIREMEN POSING WITH A HORSE-DRAWN CHEMICAL WAGON IN FRONT OF THE BERLIN FIRE STATION, C. 1910.

BERLIN POLICE DEPARTMENT PERSONNEL WITH A PADDY WAGON AND A MOTORCYCLE PATROLMAN POSING AT CITY HALL IN 1919.

A 1947 PORTRAIT OF THE BERLIN POLICE DEPARTMENT AND POLICE COMMISSION. Noteworthy in this photograph is City Police Marshall Hynes and Patrolmen Landry, Lachance, and Fabisiak.

A 1922 VIEW OF THE A.W. WALTERS FUNERAL HOME MOTORIZED FLEET OF AUTOMOBILES ON PLEASANT STREET, ESTABLISHED IN 1893.

DIRECTORS B. EDWARD BRYANT AND BERTRAND E. BRYANT OF BRYANT FUNERAL HOMES, 180 HILLSIDE AVENUE. The establishment was originally known as the A.W. Walters Funeral Home, later becoming Parker and Holmes, with the Bryant family purchasing the business in 1966.

114

MR. OSCAR F. FLEURY AT AGE 20. He was the president and founder of Fleury Funeral Homes. This portrait was taken in 1929. Mr. Fleury was once in partnership with Mr. Alfred Ruel, operating an establishment on lower Hillside Avenue. His tradition of excellent service has continued since 1938, passing on to his son-in-law, Raymond N. Patry, and most recently to his grandson, Michael A. Patry.

A 1960S VIEW OF THE FLEURY FUNERAL HOME BUILDING ON 72 HIGH STREET. It is now known as the Fleury-Patry Funeral Home under the direction of Michael A. Patry and Raymond N. Patry.

THE FLEURY FUNERAL HOME AT 497 BURGESS STREET ON THE EAST SIDE IN THE 1950S. This funeral home, which closed in 1998, was the only one of its kind on Berlin's East Side.

ARTHUR RIOUX
Licensed Embalmer

Funeral Director and Ambulance Service

Office : 511 Main Street, Berlin, N. H.
Phone 252-W

ARTHUR RIOUX FUNERAL COACHES FROM 1928. Mr. Rioux's establishment was located at the corner of Main and Cambridge Streets.

Seven

CLASSMATES OF YESTERYEAR

A SOPHISTICATED AND ELEGANT PHOTOGRAPH DEPICTING THE BERLIN HIGH SCHOOL GIRL'S BASKETBALL BEAM OF 1903. Athletics have always played a large role in the education of Berlin's youth. This philosophy is still very much in vogue today, from the hockey glories of days past, thus giving recognition to Berlin's distinction of being "Hockey Town USA," to the many state football, baseball, and basketball championships. Pictured from left to right in the above photograph are A. Haines, M. Laffin, A. Lowe, L. Coffey, L. Fancy, C. Paulson, and R. Corbett.

STUDENTS OF THE CATES HILL SCHOOLHOUSE SITUATED ON CATES HILL. The school operated from 1921 to 1934.

THE "CATES HILL SCHOOL BUS." This extended sedan was used to transport students from Cates Hill to town in the 1930s. Pictured are the Bisson, Robichaud, and Lacasse children.

THE ORIGINAL BERLIN HIGH SCHOOL IN A PEN-AND-INK SKETCH AROUND 1890. It stood on the site of the old Burgess School, which later became Notre Dame High School.

THE BERLIN HIGH SCHOOL CLASS OF 1906 BY HALLIE WILSON. It is interesting to note how small the graduating classes were at the turn of the century.

THE 1924 BERLIN HIGH SCHOOL FOOTBALL SQUAD. This was a force to be reckoned with indeed. Pictured from left to right are the following: (front row) Cordwell, Stafford, Gagne, Bartlett, Wheeler, and Lazure; (second row) Couture, McShane, Gordon, Hamel, Locke, Holt, Graves, and Atwood; (third row) Coach Thomas, G. Morin, Bernard, Stranger, Madan, L. Morin, Wagner, Snodgrass, and Manager Ryder; (back row) Bloom, M. Morin, Moore, Donovan, Taylor, and Reed.

THE BERLIN HIGH SCHOOL CLASS OF 1925, POSING BENEATH THE ENTRANCE ARCH OF THE NEW HIGH SCHOOL.

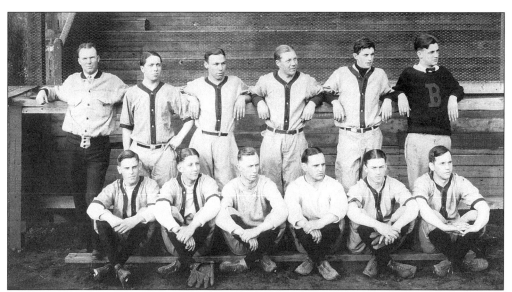

THE 1925 BERLIN HIGH SCHOOL BASEBALL TEAM IN A CLASSIC DUGOUT BACKDROP. Shown here are, from left to right, as follows: (front row) Stafford, Reid, Locke, Morin, Garneau, and Mcshane; (back row) Coach Thomas, Dumas, Couture, Pederson, Murray, and Manager Madan.

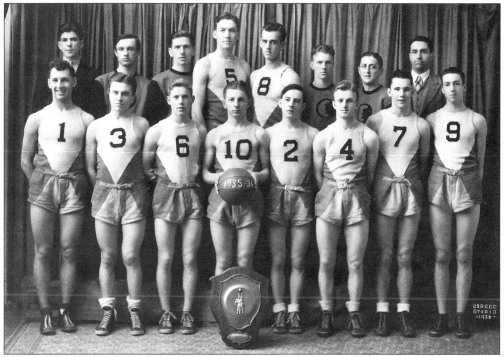

THE BERLIN HIGH SCHOOL MEN'S CHAMPIONSHIP BASKETBALL TEAM, 1935–36. Pictured from left to right are the following: (front row) A. Lavernoich, A. Kluchnick, E. Theberge, W. Savchick, Capt. L. Cryans, L. Burgess, P. Grenier, and C. Manton; (back row) Manager N. Robichaud, J. Kluchnick, N. Dale, A. Heroux, E. Davis, B. Lavernoich, R. Farrington, and Coach E.J. Garrett.

THE 1940 BERLIN HIGH SCHOOL STATE CHAMPION HOCKEY TEAM. Pictured from left to right are the following: (front row) Lafleur, Tremblay, Bouchard, Pinette, Dugas, Toussaint, and Captain Fournier; (middle row) Coach Campagna, Manager Griffin, and Roy; (back row) Jean, Nolet, Goddard, Welch, Gemmitti, and Vallieres.

THE 1966–67 GIRLS' FIELD HOCKEY TEAM AT COMMUNITY FIELD WITH STE. ANNE'S IN THE BACKGROUND. Among the young women in the first row are D. Holt, K. Sullivan, D. Perry, and D. Norton. The other young women, from left to right, are as follows: (middle row) J. Accardi, R. Johnson, A. Drouin, S. Fortier, S. St. Germaine, M. Riff, C. Warner, and E. Falardeau; (back row) K. Lessard, D. Labnon, M. York, L. Johnson, R. Mason, K. Fysh, C. Murphy, J. Belanger, D. Johnson, C. Hayes, G. Ouellette, and Coach Bradley.

THE 1944–45 BERLIN HIGH SCHOOL NORTHERN NEW ENGLAND SKI TEAM. Pictured from left to right are as follows: (front row) D. Sheridan, R. Baker, C. Oleson, Capt. G. Ricker, R. Reid, and R. Vautour; (back row) Coach B. Keough, G. Hennessey, D. Oleson, C. Lundblad, D. Beaudoin, and Manager T. Sulley.

NOTRE DAME HIGH SCHOOL'S FIRST HOCKEY TEAM IN 1944. Pictured from left to right are the following: Fr. Provost, Jean Morency, Bob Rainville, Leo Montminy, Maurice Bugeau, Raymond Dugas, Robert Rodrigue, Robert Lacroix, Paul Lepage, Husky Poirier, Jean Guy Vachon, Sonny Marois, Fernand Peloquin, Bernard Dupuis, and Fr. St.Pierre.

YOUNG LADIES AT THEIR SCHOOL DESKS AT L'ACADEMIE ST. REGIS ELEMENTARY SCHOOL IN 1934.

THE ST. REGIS ACADEMY CLASS OF 1934. Pictured with the students is Fr. Melancon. Students leaving St. Regis at this time were either destined to enter the work force with their diplomas or were to attend Berlin High School. Young men would often attend the Seminaire de Sherbrooke, with some young ladies entering religious life in Canada.

AN EIGHTH-GRADE GRADUATION PHOTOGRAPH IN FRONT OF THE ST. REGIS ENTRANCE WITH FR. DRAPEAU, 1950.

THE FIRST GRADUATING CLASS OF NOTRE DAME HIGH SCHOOL, THE CLASS OF 1943, WITH REV. OMER BOUSQUET. This graduation was noteworthy in that the high school had recently received accreditation after being in operation for less than two years.

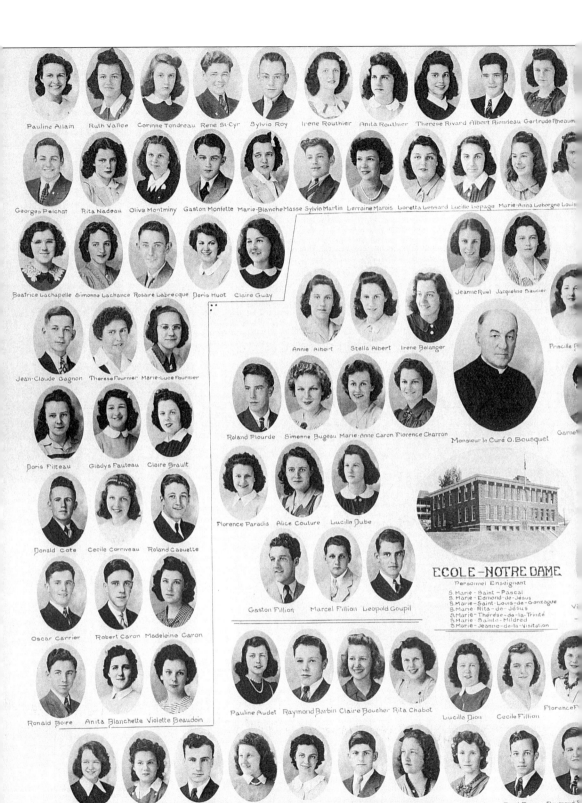

Pauline Allain Ruth Vallee Corinne Tondreau Rene St-Cyr Sylvio Roy Irene Routhier Anita Routhier Therese Rivard Albert Riendeau Gertrude Rheaum

Georges Pelchat Rita Nadeau Oliva Montminy Gaston Monfette Marie-Blanche Masse Sylvio Martin Lorraine Marois Loretta Lessard Lucille Lepage Marie-Anna Leborgne Louis

Beatrice Lachapelle Simonne Lachance Rosaire Labrecque Doris Huot Claire Guay

Jeanne Ruel Jacqueline Saucier

Jean-Claude Gagnon Therese Fournier Marie-Luce Fournier

Annie Albert Stella Albert Irene Belanger

Priscille P

Doris Filteau Gladys Fauteau Claire Brault

Roland Plourde Simonne Bugeau Marie-Anne Caron Florence Charron

Monsieur le Curé O. Bousquet

Garne

Donald Cote Cecile Corriveau Roland Caouette

Florence Paradis Alice Couture Lucille Dube

Oscar Carrier Robert Caron Madeleine Caron

Gaston Fillion Marcel Fillion Leopold Goupil

ECOLE—NOTRE DAME
Personnel Enseignant
S. Marie - Saint - Pascal
S. Marie - Edmond-de-Jésus
S. Marie - Saint-Louis-de-Gonzague
S. Marie - Rita - de - Jésus
S. Marie - Thérèse - de-la-Trinité
S. Marie - Sainte - Mildred
S. Marie - Jeanne-de-la-Visitation

Ronald Boire Anita Blanchette Violette Beaudoin

Pauline Audet Raymond Barbin Claire Boucher Rita Chabot

Lucille Dion Cecile Fillion

Florence F

Yvonnette Gosselin Jeannette Guay Hubert Lagace Jeannelle Lagassee Helene Lambert Paul Lambert Jeannette Lessard Flora Montminy Paul Pare Raymond F

Juliette Quintal Pauline Quessey Pauline Poisson Marguerite Poirier Fernand Peloquin Maurice Pelletier

Laramee Pauline Lapointe Rita Lamontagne Bella Langlois Emile Lamontagne Therese Lambert Robert Lacroix

Elizabeth Goss Jeannette Gosselin Gerard Gingras Lorraine Gilbert Mariette Gagnon

iaume Noella Bourbeau

Donat Dupuis Bernard Dupuis Nora Dugas

Cormier Pauline Cote Lucien Roy

Doris Bourque Therese Dutil Pauline Dutil

Jumont Lucille Dusseault Pauline Morneau

Frank Boucher Therese Daigle Roland Couture

oise Labrecque Maurice Morneau

Maria Berrouard Rollande Bergeron Arthur Bosa

rechette Juliette Gagnon Nora Giroux

Conrad Aube Alfred Arsenault Lucille Arguin

nte Antonia Poisson Yvette Poulin Anna-Marie Rooney Loretta Roy Beatrice St Pierre

WAGONER STUDIO

A CAMEO COLLAGE OF STUDENTS OF L'ECOLE SECONDAIRE NOTRE DAME, BERLIN, NEW HAMPSHIRE. Students appear in the center of the piece along with Monsieur le Cure Omer Bousquet Pastor of l'Ange Gardien Parish. Children from Franco-American families comprised the majority of the student body. Graduating classes of 1943 to 1945 are represented in the photograph.

127

A VINTAGE PHOTOGRAPH OF THE CHARMING BERLIN HIGH SCHOOL GIRLS' BASKETBALL TEAM OF 1923. The nautical theme, with a Charleston twist, is evident in the picture.

THE BERLIN HIGH SCHOOL BOYS BASKETBALL TEAM OF 1924. Pictured from left to right are Locke, Reed, Atwood, Stafford, Willoughby, Bloom, Sheridan, Manager Sylvain, and Coach Thomas.